Weaving NDE Threads

Cultivating Meaning and Purpose After Spiritually Transformative Experiences

A Creative Exploration of Self-Discovery and Renewal

RAQUEL RENÉ MARTIN

If found
please
kindly return to:

_____
_____
_____
_____
_____
_____

Weaving NDE Threads

Cultivating Meaning and Purpose After Spiritually Transformative Experiences

A Creative Exploration of Self-Discovery and Renewal

RAQUEL RENÉ MARTIN

2024

COPYRIGHT

CONTENTS

DAY 1: SHARING OUR STORIES

DAY 2: CREATIVE EXPRESSION

DAY 3: CULTIVATING ABUNDANCE FROM WITHIN

DAY 4: ENVISIONING YOUR FLOURISHING FUTURE

DAY 5: RECONNECTING WITH NATURE'S EMBRACE

DAY 6: UNVEILING YOUR TRANSFORMATION

DAY 7: SHARING SEEDS OF LIGHT

DAY 8: UNVEILING PATTERNS AND PROGRESS

DAY 9: UNTANGLING THE THREADS OF CURIOSITY

DAY 10: WEAVING YOUR NDE TAPESTRY INTO DAILY LIFE

PREFACE

Dear Friend,

Welcome to this heartfelt guide that I've poured my love into. I'm happy to share my journey and the insights I've gained from an extraordinary experience.

I found myself in a profound life-threatening encounter in 2023 that completely transformed my life. For 37 minutes, I was unconscious, suspended between the realms of life and death. It was an awe-inspiring moment that left an everlasting impact on me.

During that time, I glimpsed truths that surpassed anything I could have imagined. It was like peering into a hidden universe, where the mystical merged with the tangible. This experience sparked a deep sense of purpose within me and ignited a burning desire to support others who've had similar encounters.

And that's why "Weaving NDE Threads: Cultivating Meaning and Purpose After Spiritually Transformative Experiences" came to be. This guide is my way of offering support and inspiration to those who've walked a similar transformative path. It's filled with insights, practical tools, and transformative exercises—everything you need to process and integrate your own extraordinary experience.

I want you to know that you're not alone on this journey. There's a vibrant community out there, filled with individuals who've experienced similar encounters. Together, we can weave the threads of our lives into a tapestry of resilience, growth, and profound significance.

As you delve into these pages, my hope is that you'll find solace, understanding, and a renewed sense of direction. Let this guide be your companion, lighting the way as you navigate the depths of your own transformative journey.

So, find a cozy spot, dear friend, open your heart, and let's embark on this incredible adventure together.

Lots of love,

Raquel

Dedication

To all who have journeyed beyond the veil:

This dedication is for you—the brave voyagers who have glimpsed the other side. You, who in the profound silence of the near-death experience, have touched the essence of existence. Your return carries the imprints of an eternal love and a connection that defies the boundaries of the physical world.

May your stories inspire and your insights illuminate. You are the living bridges between the seen and the unseen, the reminders of a love that binds us all, transcending time and space.

With awe and reverence,
We honor your journey.

NDE?

Understanding NDEs and STEs:
The Essence of Transformation
Exploring the NuancesWithin "Weaving NDE Threads:
Cultivating Meaning and Purpose After Near-Death Experiences"

When we delve into the profound and often mysterious realm of Near-Death Experiences (NDEs) and Spiritual Transformative Experiences (STEs), we enter a space that is both deeply personal and widely diverse in interpretation and meaning.

The title of this book, "Weaving NDE Threads: Cultivating Meaning and Purpose After Spiritually Transformative Experiences," intentionally embraces a broad spectrum of these profound moments. However, it's important to recognize the nuanced distinctions that can exist between what is clinically defined as an NDE and other experiences that might more accurately be described as STEs.

In the traditional sense, an NDE occurs when a person comes close to death or reaches a state of clinical death and subsequently returns to life, often with an account of what transpired during that period of unconsciousness. These accounts typically include elements such as a feeling of peace, a sense of detachment from the body, encounters with ethereal beings or deceased loved ones, a review of one's life, and, in some cases, a reluctance to return to life. However, the term "NDE" has become more widely known and searched for among the public than "STE," which encompasses a broader range of experiences that may not be linked to a life-threatening event. STEs can include profound spiritual awakenings, mystical experiences, deep meditative states, and other transformative events that share similar life-altering impacts as NDEs. These experiences can lead to significant shifts in consciousness and alterations in one's understanding of life and existence.

For the purpose of this book, when I refer to NDEs, I am casting a wide net to include not only the classic near-death scenarios but also those transformative experiences that might align more closely with STEs. The reason for this generalized use of "NDE" is pragmatic; STE is not as widely known or researched by the general public, and those seeking information or solace regarding their experiences are more likely to come across resources and communities under the umbrella of NDE.

It's essential to appreciate that every NDE and STE is as unique as the individual who experiences it. The fabric of each story is interwoven with personal meaning, cultural backgrounds, and individual interpretations. While this book uses NDE as a generalized term, it in no way diminishes the profound nature of any spiritual or transformative experience that doesn't strictly fit the classical NDE criteria.

In the end, whether we label these moments as NDEs or STEs, the focus of "Weaving NDE Threads" is to offer support, guidance, and community to those seeking to understand and integrate these life-changing events into their lives. Through shared stories, insights, and reflections, we aim to cultivate a deeper sense of meaning and purpose that emerges from the tapestry of these extraordinary experiences.

So, as you turn the pages of this book, remember that the terminology is a bridge to a much larger conversation—one that honors the rich diversity of personal experiences and the universal quest for understanding the profound transformations they can inspire.

Welcome

Welcome NDErs, STErs and Experiencers!
Over the next 10 days, we will engage in meaningful exercises that honor where you've been while nurturing hopeful visions for your future. Our circles provide a confidential space to feel heard and heal through connection with others on similar journeys.

Day 1:
Sharing Our Stories

Today's Focus:

Verbally processing your NDE or STE experience.

Finding comfort and connection through shared stories.

Practicing active listening without judgment.

Your Goal:

- **Write Your Story:** Find a quiet space where you can reflect.
- **Write down your NDE or STE story** in as much detail as you feel comfortable sharing.
- **Share in Your Circle:** Gather with your group in a supportive circle.
- **Share a one-minute summary of your story,** focusing on key moments and emotions.
- **Listen actively to others' stories** without interrupting or giving advice.

Additional Tips:

- **Bring a journal or notebook for writing.**
- **Be mindful of your own comfort level when sharing.**
- **Respect the confidentiality of others' stories.**
- **Focus on creating a safe and supportive space for all.**

Remember: You are not alone. Your experiences are valid, and sharing them can be a powerful step in healing and understanding.

Day 1
Reflection

Day 1 Checklist

- ○ Dedicate 10 minutes of my day to check in with my Circle
- ○ Share my story.
- ○ ....
- ○ ....
- ○ ....
- ○ ....
- ○ ....
- ○ ....
- ○ ....
- ○ ....
- ○ ....
- ○ ....

Day 2:
Creative Expression

Today's Focus:

Exploring non-verbal expression of your NDE or STE experience and insights.

Uncovering hidden emotions and perspectives through art and journaling.

Discovering the joy and healing power of creative exploration.

Your Goal:

Choose your canvas: Decide whether you'd like to express yourself through art (painting, drawing, etc.), music, poetry, journaling, etc. No artistic skills are required!

Dive into your inner world: Close your eyes and take a few deep breaths. Recall your NDE or STE experience, focusing on emotions, visions, or realizations that stand out to you.

Let your creativity flow: Don't worry about creating a masterpiece! Allow your hands, words, or whatever tool you choose to guide you. Just paint, draw, write, or express whatever emerges from within.

No judgement zone: This is a safe space to explore without criticism. Let go of expectations and embrace the process.

Reflect and share (optional): If you feel comfortable, share your art with the group. You can simply describe your creative experience or offer any insights it brought you.

Additional Tips:

- Play some calming music to set the mood.
- Use materials that inspire you –
- paint, pastels, clay, markers, whatever sparks your creativity.
- Let your intuition guide you, don't overthink it.
- Embrace the messy and playful side of your imagination.
- Focus on the process of creation, not the final product.
- Remember: This is a personal journey of exploration.
- There are no right or wrong ways to express yourself. Embrace the opportunity to learn more about yourself and connect with your NDE or STE experience on a deeper level.
- Have fun and unleash your inner artist!

Day 2
Reflection

Day 2
Checklist

○ Dedicate 10 minutes of my day to check in with my Circle
....

○ Let my creativity flow
....

○ ....

○ ....

○ ....

○ ....

○ ....

○ ....

○ ....

○ ....

○ ....

○ ....

Day 3:
Cultivating Abundance from Within

Today's Focus:

Recognizing the positive shifts and insights that have blossomed since your experience.

Strengthening resilience and perspective by celebrating personal evolution.

Attuning to the joy and abundance woven into your journey.

Your Goals :

Reflect on Your NDE or STE:
- Find a quiet space, a sanctuary for reflection.
- Take a few deep breaths, allowing yourself to settle into the present moment.
- Recall your NDE or STE experience, not as a singular event, but as a catalyst for growth.
- Identify three seeds of change that have taken root and flourished since your experience. These could be inner strengths discovered, new perspectives gained, or relationships nurtured through newfound openness.

Express Your Appreciation for Growth:
- Write down each seed of change, describing how it has blossomed in your life.
- Share how these gifts have enriched your sense of self and your perspective on the world.

Consider sharing your reflections with your circle, or simply keep them in your journal as a treasure chest of personal transformation.

Additional Tips:

Create a growth log or vision board to track your blossoming strengths and aspirations.
Celebrate even the smallest steps forward, acknowledging your unwavering spirit.
Notice the joy and fulfillment that arise from recognizing your abundance.

Share your insights and growth with others, inspiring and supporting each other on your journeys.

Engage in activities that nourish your spirit, like creative expression or connecting with nature.

Remember: Your NDE or STE wasn't just a moment; it was a spark that ignited a flame of evolution within you.

Today, we celebrate the fruits of that growth, the rich landscape of your being cultivated from within.

May your heart brim with appreciation for the abundance you embody!

Day 3
Reflection

Day 3 Checklist

○ Dedicate 10 minutes of my day to check in with my Circle
....

○ Write my three seeds of change
....

○
....

○
....

○
....

○
....

○
....

○
....

○
....

○
....

○
....

○
....

○
....

Day 4:
Envisioning Your Flourishing Future

Today's Focus:

Cultivating hope and motivation by visualizing a positive future.

Aligning your actions with your deepest aspirations and values.

Empowering yourself to create a life that truly resonates with your soul.

Your Goals:

Reflect on Your NDE or STE Insights:

- **Find a quiet space where you can dream freely.**
- **Recall the insights and perspectives gained during your NDE or STE.**
- **Consider how these insights have shifted your priorities and values.**
- **Ask yourself: What kind of life feels most aligned with who you are now?**

Paint Your Future Vision:

- **Close your eyes and imagine a future where you're thriving, guided by your wisdom.**
- **Describe this vision in detail, using all your senses.**
- **What are you doing? Where are you living? Who's by your side? How do you feel?**
- **Write down this vision, creating a vivid portrait of your desired future.**

Map Out Your Steps:

- **Identify a few concrete steps you can take towards this vision.**
- **These could be small daily actions or larger goals to work towards.**
- **Consider what resources, support, or skills you might need to develop.**
- **Create a plan that feels both inspiring and attainable.**

Additional Tips:

- **Visualize your future daily, reinforcing its clarity and possibility.**

- **Set realistic but meaningful goals that create momentum.**

- **Celebrate your progress, no matter how small the steps.**

- **Surround yourself with people who support your vision.**

- **Embrace challenges as opportunities for growth and learning.**

- **Remember, your experience has illuminated a path of purpose and meaning. Trust your heart's compass to guide you towards a fulfilling future.**

May you envision a future that fills you with hope, purpose, and boundless possibility!

Day 4
Reflection

Day 4
Checklist

◯ Dedicate 10 minutes of my day to check in with my Circle
....

◯ Create a vivid vision of my flourishing future
....

◯
....

◯
....

◯
....

◯
....

◯
....

◯
....

◯
....

◯
....

◯
....

◯
....

Day 5:
Reconnecting with Nature's Embrace

Today's Focus:

Experiencing the restorative power of nature.

Allowing the natural world to soothe and replenish your being.

Strengthening your connection with the Earth and its cycles.

Your Goals:

Choose Your Nature Sanctuary:
- Select an outdoor space that resonates with you: a park, forest, beach, garden, or even a quiet spot in your backyard.
- Prioritize a place that feels calming and inviting, where you can fully immerse yourself in the natural surroundings.

Engage Your Senses:
- As you enter your chosen space, take a few deep breaths and consciously tune into your senses.
- Notice the sights, sounds, smells, and textures of nature around you.
- Feel the warmth of the sun, the gentle breeze, or the soft earth beneath your feet.
- Allow yourself to become fully present in this moment, enveloped by nature's embrace.

Find Harmony in Motion:
> Engage in an activity that allows you to connect with nature in a way that feels enjoyable and grounding.

> **Some ideas include:**
- Walking or hiking amidst the trees, noticing the vibrant life around you,
- Sitting quietly by a flowing stream, observing the water's soothing rhythm.
- Practicing yoga or meditation in a peaceful meadow, surrounded by the beauty of nature.
- Creating art inspired by the natural elements, such as painting, photography, or journaling.

Additional Tips:

- Leave your electronic devices behind, allowing yourself to fully disconnect from the digital world.

- Invite a friend or loved one to join you, sharing the experience and deepening your connection with each other.

- Practice mindfulness as you explore nature, focusing on the present moment and noticing the small details that bring you joy.

- Express gratitude for the gifts of nature, acknowledging its power to heal and restore.

Remember: Nature is a wise and compassionate teacher. It offers us solace, rejuvenation, and a sense of belonging to something greater than ourselves.

May this day's journey bring you peace, grounding, and a renewed connection with the natural world.

Day 5
Reflection

Day 5
Checklist

◯ Dedicate 10 minutes of my day to check in with my Circle
....

◯ Enjoy nature.
....

◯
....

◯
....

◯
....

◯
....

◯
....

◯
....

◯
....

◯
....

◯
....

◯
....

Day 6:
Unveiling Your Transformation

Today's Focus:

Recognizing and appreciating the transformative impact of your NDE on your perspectives.

Sharing insights and learnings to expand understanding

and deepen connections within the group.

Reflecting on how these shifts have influenced your relationships,

career choices, and sense of purpose.

Your Goals:

Contemplate Your Changed Landscape:
- Find a quiet space for introspection. Take a few deep breaths and allow yourself to settle into the present moment. Recall your NDE experience and the ways it has impacted your thinking and understanding of the world.
- Consider one specific area where your perspective has shifted significantly since your experience. This could be related to life, death, relationships, spirituality, or anything else that feels relevant.

Map Your Growth Trajectory:
- Write down your chosen area of perspective shift and describe how it has changed. Share how this shift has influenced your actions, decisions, and overall approach to life.
- Identify specific examples of how this new perspective has played out in your relationships, career, or sense of purpose.

Connect Through Shared Transformation:
- Gather with your circle and share your reflections on perspective shift.
- Listen actively to others' stories, noticing the common threads and unique personal journeys.
- Discuss how these shared experiences can contribute to a deeper understanding of ourselves and each other.

Additional Tips:

- Encourage a safe and open space for honest sharing without judgment.

- Appreciate the diversity of perspectives within the group, recognizing that each experience is unique.

- Consider using metaphors or visual aids to illustrate your perspective shifts.

- Reflect on how learning from each other's transformation can empower your own continued growth.

Remember: Your experience has gifted you with a new lens through which to view the world. Today, we celebrate the beauty and power of those shifts, recognizing how they enrich your own journey and strengthen the bonds within your community.

May your shared exploration of transformation illuminate your path and inspire deeper connections!

Day 6
Reflection

Day 6
Checklist

○ Dedicate 10 minutes of my day to check in with my Circle
....

○
....

○
....

○
....

○
....

○
....

○
....

○
....

○
....

○
....

○
....

○
....

Day 7:
Sharing Seeds of Light

Today's Focus:

Identifying the small but powerful sparks of inspiration that fuel your personal growth.

Sharing these inspirations with the group to nourish one another's journeys.

Recognizing the interconnectedness of our experiences

and the collective power of positive influence.

Your Goals:

Uncover Your Daily Spark:

Take a few moments of quiet reflection in your chosen space. Think about your day-to-day life. What small moments, encounters, or realizations bring you joy, ignite your purpose, or encourage you to be a better person? This "daily spark" could be anything from a beautiful sunrise to a kind word received, a creative breakthrough, or a moment of deep connection.

Nurture Your Seed:

Write down your chosen daily spark, describing it in detail and how it impacts your outlook or motivates your actions. Consider how this spark connects to the insights gained during your NDE and your overall vision for the future.

Share Your Light:

- Gather with your circle and share your daily spark with everyone.
- Listen attentively as others share their own inspirations, noticing the common threads and unique ways each person finds meaning in their day-to-day lives.
- Discuss how these shared sparks of inspiration can contribute to a broader sense of hope, motivation, and interconnectedness within the group.

Additional Tips:

- Create a beautiful "inspiration jar" to collect written reflections or symbolic representations of your daily sparks.

- Encourage active listening and appreciation for each other's unique perspectives.

- Consider incorporating elements of mindfulness or gratitude into your daily lives to cultivate ongoing inspiration.

- Remember, even the smallest spark can ignite a fire of possibility. By sharing our lights, we illuminate the path for ourselves and each other.

May your day be filled with moments that ignite your spirit and inspire you to share your inner radiance with the world!

Day 7
Reflection

Day 7
Checklist

○ Dedicate 10 minutes of my day to check in with my Circle

○

○

○

○

○

○

○

○

○

○

○

○

Day 8:
Unveiling Patterns and Progress

Today's Focus:

Reflecting on key moments and patterns from throughout your life pre- and post-NDE.

Identifying areas of personal growth and progress in chosen aspects of your life.

Recognizing the continuity and transformative power

of your NDE experience within your life's narrative.

Your Goals:

Choose Your Lens:
- Select an area of your life you'd like to explore through the lens of your experience: relationships, career, creativity, spirituality, or any other area that feels significant.
- Briefly recall key moments or patterns within this chosen area before your NDE or STE, noting themes, challenges, and aspirations.

Trace Your Transformation:
- Reflect on how your experience has impacted this chosen area of your life.

- Identify specific moments, realizations, or shifts in perspective that have contributed to your growth and ongoing transformation.

- Consider tangible actions, choices, or changes you've made since your NDE or STE that reflect the insights gained.

Weave the Threads Together:
- Write down your reflections, creating a mini-narrative that weaves together key moments pre- and post-NDE within your chosen area of life.
- Highlight the continuity of your journey while celebrating the transformative power of your NDE experience.

Share Your Tapestry:
- Gather with your circle and share your mini-narrative, offering glimpses into your chosen area of life and how it has evolved post-NDE.
- Listen actively to others' stories, noticing common threads and unique paths of personal growth.
- Discuss how these shared reflections can contribute to a deeper understanding of ourselves and each other's ongoing journeys.

Additional Tips:

- Consider using visualization techniques to vividly recall key moments from your life.

- Create a timeline or collage to visually represent your personal growth and evolving patterns.

- Be open to unexpected insights and celebrate the small yet significant shifts within your life's tapestry.

- Remember, your NDE is just one thread woven into the rich fabric of your being. Today, we celebrate the beauty and complexity of your ongoing transformation.

May your exploration of life's tapestry reveal the power of your Experience and inspire you to embrace the ever-evolving masterpiece of your existence!

Day 8
Reflection

Day 8
Checklist

○ Dedicate 10 minutes of my day to check in with my Circle
....

○ ....

○ ....

○ ....

○ ....

○ ....

○ ....

○ ....

○ ....

○ ....

○ ....

○ ....

Day 9:
Untangling the Threads of Curiosity

Today's Focus:

Bringing to light lingering questions, uncertainties, and curiosities arising from your NDEs.

Exploring these questions through open dialogue and

diverse perspectives within the group.

Seeking not definitive answers, but deeper understanding,

acceptance, and a sense of closure.

Your Goals:

Unveil Your Wonder:
- Take some quiet time for introspection. Reflect on your NDE experience and identify any questions, uncertainties, or areas of curiosity that still linger within you. These can be related to specific details, interpretations, or broader existential questions.

Share Your Threads:
- Gather with your circle and create a safe space for honest and open expression.
- One by one, share your lingering questions or curiosities about your NDEs.
- Listen actively and non-judgmentally to others' inquiries.

Weave the Answers:
- Engage in open dialogue as a group, exploring each other's questions with respect and curiosity.
- Remember, no one answer holds the absolute truth. Seek to share insights, personal experiences, and diverse perspectives that might shed light on each other's inquiries.
- The goal is not to find definitive answers, but to feel heard, accepted, and supported in your questioning.

Embracing Closure:
- Reflect on the experience of sharing and exploring your questions. Have any insights emerged? Do you feel a sense of clarity, acceptance, or simply deeper understanding of your Experience?
- Recognize that some questions may remain unanswered, and that's okay. Embrace the mystery and accept that the journey of discovery is ongoing.

Additional Tips:

- **Encourage creativity in expressing your questions, perhaps through writing, drawing, or metaphors.**

- **Acknowledge the vulnerability and courage it takes to share your uncertainties.**

- **Celebrate the richness of diverse perspectives and the power of community in navigating the unknown.**

- **Remember, your questioning is valid and worthy of exploration. Let go of the need for definitive answers and embrace the wisdom of open-mindedness.**

May your exploration of lingering questions bring closure, understanding, and a renewed sense of peace on your journey.

Day 9
Reflection

Day 9
Checklist

○ Dedicate 10 minutes of my day to check in with my Circle

....

○

....

○

....

○

....

○

....

○

....

○

....

○

....

○

....

○

....

○

....

○

....

Day 10:
Weaving Your NDE Tapestry into Daily Life

Today's Focus:

Reflecting on and celebrating the personal growth,

insights, and shifts in perspective gained throughout the past 10 days.

Identifying tangible ways to integrate the wisdom and lessons learned from your

Experience into your everyday life. Sharing your integration plans and visions for the future

with your circle, offering mutual support and inspiration.

Your Goals:

Harvest Your Treasure Map:
Take some quiet time to revisit your reflections and experiences from the past nine days. Identify the key insights, realizations, and shifts in perspective that have resonated most deeply with you throughout these ten days. Think of these as precious pearls or guiding stars on your life's journey.

Weaving Into the Fabric:
With your "treasure map" in hand, consider specific actions, practices, or intentions you can incorporate into your daily life to keep the light of your Experience alive. This could be anything from implementing a new mindfulness practice to prioritizing a cherished relationship differently or pursuing a long-held creative dream.

Additional Tips:

- Encourage creativity in expressing your integration plans, perhaps through journaling, drawing, or creating personal affirmations.

- Celebrate small steps and acknowledge the ongoing process of integrating your NDE or STE learnings.

- Remember, there is no single "right" way to integrate your experience.

- Trust your intuition and follow the path that feels most authentic to you.

- As you step out into the world after this course, carry the knowledge that you are not alone. You have built a supportive community with shared experiences and a commitment to living a life transformed by your Experience.

May your tapestry of daily life continue to be enriched by the threads of your Experiences, leading you to ever-greater peace, purpose, and connection!

Day 10
Reflection

Day 10 Checklist

○ Dedicate 10 minutes of my day to check in with my Circle
....

○
....

○
....

○
....

○
....

○
....

○
....

○
....

○
....

○
....

○
....

○
....

○
....

Congratulations, Weaver of Light!

You've walked through ten days of profound exploration, unveiling the threads of your NDE and weaving them into the tapestry of your being. Through introspection, creativity, and connection, you've embarked on a magnificent journey of transformation.

Reflect and Celebrate:

- Let the echoes of your NDE reverberate in your heart. Remember the awe-inspiring glimpses, the whispers of wisdom, and the boundless love you encountered.
- Trace the threads you've woven. Acknowledge the shifts in your perspective, the blossoming of your purpose, and the newfound strength you hold within.
- Celebrate your courage to embark on this journey, your openness to embrace the unknown, and your commitment to weaving a tapestry of meaning and light.

Carry the Light Forward:

- Remember, the journey doesn't end here. Keep your notebook by your side, a constant companion for reflection and creative expression.
- Let the lessons learned guide your steps. Face challenges with newfound compassion and wisdom, knowing you are part of a vast and interconnected universe.
- Share your light with others. Inspire those around you with your story, offer support and guidance, and continue weaving the tapestry of a brighter future, together.

Remember, Dear Weaver:

- You are a vessel of light, forever touched by the transformative power of your NDE.
- You are a masterpiece in the making, constantly evolving and weaving your unique story into the grand tapestry of existence.
- You are an agent of change, empowered to illuminate the world with your wisdom and compassion.

May your journey be filled with ever-unfolding wonder, abundant love, and a radiant purpose that shines beyond time itself.

Congratulations again, and may your tapestry forever shimmer with the threads of your NDE light!

Your paragraph text

In Proud Recognition

of

Completion of Weaving NDE Threads

In celebrating your completion of the "Weaving NDE Threads" 10-day program, this certificate is both a recognition and a reminder:

This certificate acknowledges your:

Open Heart: You've navigated the emotional depths and emerged with a spirit of empathy and connection.

Curious Mind: Your quest for understanding has led to profound insights and an enriched sense of self-awareness.

Present Moment: Embracing the here and now, you've found peace beyond the confines of past and future.

Creative Spark: Your individuality has shone brightly, contributing your distinct voice and vision to our collective canvas.

May this certificate serve as a beacon to continue cultivating these transformative gifts on your ongoing journey towards fulfillment and happiness.

Date

RQLRN

Name

About the Creator

Embark on a journey where the fabric of life is re-threaded with hope, understanding, and community. I am Raquel, not only a CEO, mother, and grandmother, but also a kindred spirit who has traversed the veil between life and death.

My tapestry is rich with contrasts. At 16, I teetered on the brink of mortality due to bacterial meningitis, but a mystical communion with my ancestral guardians bestowed upon me a second lease on life.

Yet, this brush with the eternal is but one thread among many. The tapestry of my life encompasses a foray into ancestral healing arts during my twenties, the entrepreneurial spirit of launching successful piercing studios, and later, a deep dive into the realms of art, music, and culture. My forties saw me don a scientist's cloak, exploring the intricacies of microbiology and endocrinology.

Now, I stand at the confluence of science and spirituality, weaving together a digital sanctuary for those touched by the profound experience of a near-death encounter.

My resilience is a testament to life's tapestry, enduring through the challenges of multiple sclerosis. More recently, an epilepsy-induced near-death experience unfolded a new chapter, inspiring me to craft the workbook, "Weaving NDE Threads: Cultivating Meaning and Purpose After Your Near Death Experience." Here, we can unravel the complexities of your NDE, stitching them into a vibrant quilt of insight and purpose.

With open arms, I invite you to join me, not as distant healers, but as warriors of the same fabric. My vision is to cultivate RQLRN, a sanctuary for 1000 souls by January 1st, 2025. A community where the aftermath of NDEs forms the cornerstone of our shared narrative, fostering healing and growth.

How may I serve you on this path?

Safe Space: Here, every voice resonates, and every story is honored. Diversity in thought and life's mosaic is our collective strength.

Further Reading

Classics and Pioneering Work:
Life After Life by Raymond Moody:
The foundational text, outlining common NDE themes and pioneering research.

Memories of a Future Home by Dr. Pim van Lommel:
A scientific study providing compelling evidence for the reality of NDEs.

Personal Transformation and Integration:
Dying to Be Me by Anita Moorjani:
A powerful story of healing and rediscovering inner joy after a terminal illness and NDE.

Embracing the Light by Emily Williams Hofmann:
A practical guide for integrating NDE insights into daily life,
focusing on purpose and emotional well-being.

Spiritual and Philosophical Explorations:
Man's Search for Meaning by Viktor Frankl:
A Holocaust survivor's reflections on finding meaning and purpose in life,
resonates with NDE themes.

The Untethered Soul by Michael A. Singer:
Explores the true nature of consciousness and transcending limitations for a joyful life.

Creative Expression and Storytelling:
The Road Less Traveled by M. Scott Peck:
A spiritual guide exploring personal growth, responsibility, and embracing life's challenges.

Big Magic by Elizabeth Gilbert:
A creative manifesto encouraging readers to pursue their passions and overcome fear,
relevant to artistic expression of NDE experiences.

Emerging Voices and Unique Perspectives:
Beyond the Veil by Cherie Moraga:
A Latina author's exploration of her NDE through a cultural and social justice lens.

Connect with Us on Social Media

UNLEASH YOUR CREATIVITY AND SHARE THE LOVE! WE'D BE THRILLED TO SEE HOW YOU BRING YOUR WEAVING NDE THREADS JOURNEY TO LIFE.

TAG US IN YOUR POSTS AND FOLLOW OUR JOURNEY FOR MORE INSPIRING CONTENT ON YOUTUBE AND TIKTOK.
✹ FOLLOW AND TAG US! ✹
TIKTOK: @RQLRN
YOUTUBE: RQLRN

STAY CONNECTED, GET INSPIRED, AND BECOME A PART OF OUR GROWING COMMUNITY!

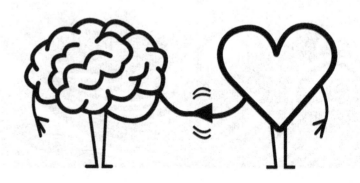

Books
by
RQLRN
Now on Amazon

Weaving NDE Threads:
Cultivating Meaning and Purpose After Near Death Experiences
by Raquel René Martin

A Mystical Account of Seizures and Transcendence
by Raquel René Martin

Your Exclusive Invitation: Weaving NDE Threads Circle

Embrace this special opportunity designed just for our readers. By scanning the QR code below, you're taking a step toward enriching your mindfulness practice with a community that understands and supports your journey. It's our gift to you—a chance to join the Weaving NDE Threads Circle and enjoy 10 days of guided connection and personal growth at no cost.

How to Use the QR Code:

1. Open the camera app on your smartphone or QR code scanner.
2. Point your camera at the QR code below and follow the prompt to open your email app.
3. Your email will be pre-addressed with the subject "Join the Harmony Mind Renewal Circle". Feel free to add a personal message if you like!
4. Send the email, and we'll respond with your invitation to the circle.